Dark Light Productions
May Those Who Seek The Truth Be Found...
Dark Light
Productions
Dark Light Productions, Lighting The Path...
I0839746

The Mental Health Scam

It seems as though at all points in history there comes a time when a disease sets in upon a society that is fear based and delusional but is none the less accepted as the norm and becomes an   new but unidentified form of oppression. What seems like the cure is actually the cause in some instances but the confusion surrounding the truth of matters disotrts the visionary from seeing a proper perspective. This is sadly what is happening again today in the same way that all oppression takes place, when a religion is considered to be a science as opposed to being a belief system. Today that oppression is being done agressivtey by the religion of Psychology while being endorsed by the state to imprison shamans based on the premise that change to their design is dangerous, and thus they promote false dialouge and brainwash the public.

To start our investigation into this backwards satanic oriented religion, meaning one that seeks to gain power through means of sacrafice as opposed to realization, by growing by means of ignorance as opposed to righteousness, we will look into the concept of it being a religion. When i say to most people that Psychology is a Religion they seem to gasp in fear as their perception of reality is shaken in a way that they know is true but will continue to deny. It is a split personality syndrome promoted as means to turn people against each other and promtoe fasle truths by means of doubt. When one truly looks into Psychology they will find that it is an opinion based belief system that follows the same teachings as relgions but leaves out the concept of God. Opinions, as educated as they may be, are not facts. There is no test that proves any mental illness, none what so ever, and the chemical imbalance theory is proven wrong again and again, so why cling to it as if it helps people?

To answer this question we must not pecieve the religion of Psychyology as being comparable to any health system for the real body, we must percieve it as it truly is, a business model. When we realize that the religion actually accepts it own faults, and knows they are wrong, but still promotes them anyways, we then know that what we are working with is a system that is benefiting both the good and the bad within that system, and so by cohesive function we create a evil system. Angels do not work with Demons, and yet they are. This means both sides are benefiting from the suffering of others and one side gets to play the savior role while the other plays the oppressor role, while in the end it is a set up all along to those who are caught in the middle, those who become targets by the cult of Psychology, which takes over in secret by forming alliances between the good and the bad, making it seem like a compromise when in truth it is a deceptive business model.

To provide more evidence for my case i would like to point to the suppossed mental diseases that cannot be proven by any tests. I have been through the system and this comes from first hand experience, what the religion of psychology teaches one to do is to blame the self instead of love the self, it is backwards. Instead of seeing an abnormality as something possibly divine they see abnomralities as diseases that should be cured. This promotes self blame for disorders that cannot be proven either way. They take doubt and sway it to the side of disease, whcich promotes oppression rather than understanding, and i think this is being done on purpose. If one self blames this will create a downwards cycle which will keep them thinking something is wrong with them when possibly it was an environmental circumstance causing an issue to arise at a precise moment in time as opposed to a long term disorder. If one blames the self they never see the truth, and they circle to saviors.

By making a person believe they have a false disorder it allows one to utilize that doubt to become their savior and get their egos fed which is part of the heirarchy business model of Psychology, it also involves Psycholgy payments, thus why the good and bad work together. The good are paid in deceptive praise and the bad get money from the insurances and payments to be part of the religion, as well as the drugs they force on to people for diseases that cannot be proven. This is the promotion of sacrament by forced means and communion not with God, as Psychology leaves God out, but communion with the disorder one is treating. Medications feed demons when they are not focused on being healed by God, and Psychologies demons are known as Anxiety, Depression, Schizophrenia, Schizo Affective, Bipolar, etc... Demons only grow in the dark, thus making one believe in a false illness, while promoting sacrament use towards the illness, will grow the demon even more, not less. Business

We then have support groups and counseling which is the equivilent of confession in religion except once again the concept of God is gone and so the ego of the Psychologist, or false God, is being fed by playing the role of God. This is to promote deciet and doubt so that the God keeps their worshippers, so the psychologists keeps their patients, so the business gets paid. I have been through these classes of the religion of psychology and they teach the trinity, the elements, the tree of life, and other well known religious concepts, but they teach them backwards, so that the self stays the blame point and the focus stays on salvation by understanding their diagnosis which is actually not a true disease, it cannot be proven, and they know this. Thus we have the snake talk and backwards tounge of the Psychologists who are truly performing rituals when their clients visit them and are taking advantage of the trust given to them by those seeking true help.

As much as i would like to say the development of the religion of Psychology was done so that a universal religion was formed for peace, what i see in the psychwards is complete oppression, not peace by any means. I do not see healing, i see repeat customers looking for help from false shamans looking to gain power. And this is the next part of why the mental health industry scam is going on, and that is because of shamanism. Those is power are threatened by the shaman's ability to free people and heal people for free, and so to take out any and all forms of competition Psychology was created as a religion promoted as a science to turn the public against the shaman. The Shaman is no longer the spiritual healer, the Shaman is now the Schizophrenic with a disorder or disease. A propganda based move to turn people against their own saviors by making it appear as though those saviors are dangerous people when in fact it is purposeful provoktion.

Programs have been said to have been developed by those in power that allow them to target shamans by means of using what is called remote viewing. This means that shamans who can remote view are targetting shamans who can remote view but don't know what they are. This seems to be the common theme is all the psych wards. People are convinced of false truths given to them so that they do not think they are the ones who distorted reality or can distort reality. This is done to oppress the shamans not controlled by the religion of psychology because it threatens their business model, the Shaman can reveal the truth. And so we have teams that the government has set up that watch for shamans and then target them to oppress them in jails or mental institutions so that they cannot realize their full potentials. I have witnessed this persecution first hand and can attest to it, it is called gang stalking and they harass by means of technology and psychological set ups, scripts.

But there is another reason the Shaman is being targeted which has to do with a business model but one which most can't understand, which is the developement of mental disorders as a means of infectious warfare through behavioral codes and relations. If a shaman is targeted in secret, by technological means, and is put in set up situations, what will begin to happen is that a demon will start to grow in the darkness within the Shaman because the shaman is being promoted to self blame when they are being targeted. Those who are targeting are building and designing demons within people so that those people, shamans, are able to infect others with behavioral codes that are contagious. If they say happiness is contagious then these made up diseases are too, but again they must be built in the dark. This then turns everyone against the Shaman, even the shaman themselves sometimes, and the new disorder is born, the new way to make money.

This ties into why the government is involved, it is the development of psychological warfare tools in individuals which can be passed and promoted as infections onto political targets. Imagine being able to infect the president with the demon depression, and then think about how this would enable others to be able to sway decisions. Think about how the president could use this knowledge to infect other diplomats by means of a handshake. And now the truth comes to light, it is a military project designed to use civilians as a means to develop mental weapons while hiding behind the false science of psychology, which is truly a religion. A great deception that the public falls for everytime. The Christians did it during their persecutions and witch trials, and now it is being done again. How many times does the same thing in history have to occur before people wake up to see that being involved in groups with idealizations towards false realities is the problem?

And this brings us to our next deduction about psychology, that it in reality is demon worship and demonology at practice being endorsed by the state to where there is supposed to be seperation of state and religion. This would mean the state has adopted Atheism as its religion, or the religion that excludes God, Psychology, which has allowed for the infection of demonology as a means for business pursuits to occurr. What was meant to be good is now bad, it is the same as every other form of persecution throughout history and yet it is being ignored. People are being 302'd against their will and sent to psychwards that put them on medications that screw them up for life. I was sent to a psychward, everyone was overmedicated, i suffered permanent damgage from malpractice which no one will acknowledge, and this seems to be a regular thing. The acceptance of demonlogy has become the norm for society, and this is placing individuals in harms way.

To site a bit of evidence on my claims against psychology and its religious persecutions i would like to talk about the current group that is trying to help improve the mental health stigmas and help patients in need to find a better approach, or so they claim. But when you look into the funding of the group called NAMI, you will find that 75% of their funding comes from pharmaceutical companies! 75%! That means they are owned by those who they are supposed to be watchdogs over. That right there is nothing more than a scam meant to spread their relgious terminology by any means necessary. To say you are helping the victims of metal health abuses and then be funded by the ones who abused those people, and made a profit from abusing those people, and now will continue to make a profit off of their continued need for care, is a complete scam and rip off. Anyone who cannot see that is blind to what is happeninig in America, and the world.

To explain how the psychiatric world is oppressing the shaman one needs to understand the concept of dark light and its functions with God's perception of the world. Most all of the drugs they put people on lower dopamine. Lowering dopamine lowers one's ability to illuminate their inner third eye pineal gland, which is like a black light in the body. By dimming this light what they are doing is lowering the shamans ability to see inside of their cave, to see their memories on the 5ht circuit. It is quite literally dimming the lights. Why do you think you see everyone in psychwards continually drinking coffee? It is because they are having their dopamine receptors systematically destroyed. The reason they are doing this is to control creative force and output. They turn some on, and some off, and this creates either a need for more creation from God or a need for less creation from God. They are using the Shaman against God's wishes.

By controlling the shaman they are tricking God into providing more creation, and then they let this flow come through certain individuals, which they are controlling in order to steal from the Shaman by means of altered perceptions. The Shaman then is told they are insane, placed on drugs again to dim their lights in the hopes they forget, and then they repeat or keep watch and medicated. The Shamans serve as God's servants of light and are suppossed to bring technology of the divine down to earth from the heavens above as gifts. But not all can be shamans, and so the shamans are usually revered and loved and given gifts of adornements to surivie, but in the United States Shamans are being used and then told they are crazy, abused in psywards and damaged for life after the entire cycle, and society is allowing this due to the false lie that Psychology is a science and not a religion. Evil is allowed to prevail in the face of ignorance.

What we need to understand as a culture is that behaviors are not diseases, they are behaviors. And yes some need dealt with in certain ways, but to start labelling people as having disorders removes the label of human from them and creates a heirarchy system where there should be love. Love heals behaviors, a change of environment that promotes more love heals behaviors that are considered bad because there are no behaviors that are bad, only individuals in places that are bad. To not understand this and blame the individual is a crime against the very element of being human, the very thing that allowed humanity to get to the pinnacle point that it has gotten to. When i got treated at a wellness clinic, involuntarially, i asked if they agreed that behaviors were not diseases, and then i was taught a class about understanding your diagnosis and disorder. What? So my behavior is not a disease but i need to understand it as such? Snake talk.

In cultures past they taught that people who were considered different were touched by the divine, as long as they were not too disabled to be seen as disabled. This is the way we need to view things in modern times. During my studies into shamanism I've come to find that altered states of perceptions are glimpses into different dimensions of understandning, different colors of clarity, and if we can learn to contol these gifts we can problem solve in different ways, like so:

Conscious Observation
Focused Intent
Unified Whole
Balanced Structure
Experience Of
Creative Measurements
Mystical Contemplations
Knowledge Known
Creative Force

Knowing how the shaman works allows one to understand mental disorders better. People who are hallucinating are increasing alpha brain waves while their eyes are open and thus they are dipping down into the distortions of the water, of the low self world. This is not something everyone can do and is a form of contact with a spirit guide. When this occurs a person should accpet the blessings they are to recieve and close their eyes. This separates their mind from their body by polarity and they rise up into beta, possibly gamma heaven. This is why these trance states are gifts if taught how to properly be used, not everyone is granted access to heaven or can find a way to get there. Now the spontaneousness needs controlled in certain cases but that begins with the understanding that it is a gift and not a curse. Those who see what others can't are sometimes looking in doorways that others just are not allowed to look through, thus the shaman brings down the word of God.

The religion of psychology wants to silence and use the word of God for profit, and this will only backfire on all those whose souls accept the false relgion as true and persecute their brothers and sisters under the name of false dogmas and lies promoted as a pyramid scheme to make money. Most people that i have talked to in the psych wards feel as though their families are involved in their persecution. Are shamans able to be identified at birth and thus families are being given kickbacks from pharmaceutical companies to oppress their own children? If you talk long enough to people who can still make sense in the psych ward this is how it seems, and this is how i feel my excperience is going as well. If this is so then the human race should be ashamed of itself for what it is doing to its people. To fear what you don't understand is misguided and foolish. For families to turn on their loved ones for profit is disgusting.

In my eyes shcizophrenia is linked to multiple personality disorder by means of spirit guides that cross frequency channels in order to heal an individual by returning back through to the quatum world at the site of chromosome damage in attempt to heal a person by internally raising their dark light. In order for a psyche takeover or a hallucination to occur all the spirit guides must agree to open a channel from the quantum world that matches a personality trait that does not damage the person they are guiding. If a specific point needs healed a psyche takeover occurrs and a personality assigned to a specific DNA portion is sent through to cause the person to get into a different mode of thought, a different dark light color, so that proper healing can take place, to which then the spirit guide enters back through its channel. A hallucination is an attempt at all body healing by means of adrenaline dark light.

With a hallucination all of the spirit guides, or multiple personalities, open the same channel and all come through together in order to have the power to form a hallucination that is focused upon a memory that will aid in healing what needs healed the most. A hallucination is a combined effort at healing. Adrenaline is then raised in the body from the hallucination so that dark light rises. If a person learns to close their eyes and know it is their spirit guides healing them this would seperate their minds from their bodies and thus allow complete healing to occurr, without resistance. The guides would pass back through their perspective frequencies and heal chromosomes and repair DNA structures. Now, after a shaman explains the truth, can you see why the ancient cultures saw people with these "disorders" as having gifts? The potential workings to be able to affect reality comes to light only if ones eyes are open to understanding the truth.

It seems to me that all of these disorders arise from a form of multiple personalities in one form or another. It is the splitting of the psyche which causes disease and psychological problems. These psychological problems are attempts at fixing diseases that are caused by the splitting of personalities by believing in false truths, like that Psychology is not a religion, or that one is to blame for their behaviors. I can see it everywhere throughout politics to sports events. People are intentionally choosing to split their personalities when usually both sides have something good to offer, yet we are told to choose one or the other, republican or democrat. Our mind knows the truth but our body accepts a lie, and so our mind tries to heal our body by creating spiritual guides which if misunderstood can turn into psychological disorders, thus preventing the guides from healing the person and keeping them in a cycle of sickness that is truly a blessing to behold.

Dark Light Productions

The human has forgotten how much of a marvellous creation it truly is. The human does not see itself as a reflection of the love of God but as the discord of darkness where badness dwells. We need to promote a society that teaches us to love thy self rather than blame ourselves because in the end no one is to blame but ignorance.